150 YEARS

OF

CANADA

Year-by-Year
Fascinating Facts

A.H. Jackson

BLUE
BIKE
BOOKS

The Publisher: Blue Bike Books

Website: www.bluebikebooks.com

Library and Archives Canada Cataloguing in Publication

Jackson, A. H., 1944-, author
150 years of Canada / A.H. Jackson.

ISBN 978-1-926700-78-6 (softcover)

1. Canada–Miscellanea. 2. Canada–History–Miscellanea.
I. Title. II. Title: One hundred and fifty years of Canada.
III. Title: One hundred fifty years of Canada.

FC60.J33 2017   971.002   C2017-902760-3

Project Director: Peter Boer
Project Editor: Sheila Cooke
All illustrations are by Roger Garcia, Peter Tyler, Graham Johnson, Patrick Hénaff, Craig Howrie or Djordje Todorovic except the following, courtesy Thinkstock: p. 57, Creative_Outlet; pp. 27, 107, 132, 140b, 154, Dynamic Graphics; p. 147, Erie; p. 156, Jupiterimages; and p. 83, Vera Sever: 83.
Cover Image: belekekin/Thinkstock; hanohiki/Thinkstock

Produced with the assistance of the Government of Alberta, Alberta Media Fund.

Alberta
Government

We acknowledge the financial support of the Government of Canada.

Funded by the Government of Canada
Financé par le gouvernement du Canada | **Canadä**

PC: 32

CONTENTS

INTRODUCTION

This book highlights yearly happenings in Canada from Confederation in 1867 to the 150-year celebration in 2017: Canada's sesquicentennial.

Up to the year of Confederation, much had been happening in British North America and in the United States to the south. Following the American Civil War of 1861–1865, residents of the British colonies feared American annexation and expansion, particularly after the U.S. purchase of Alaska in 1867. Those in British North America also recognized Britain's increasing reluctance to defend its colonies, and the solution seemed to be strength in unity.

In September 1864, Charlottetown, Prince Edward Island, hosted a conference to discuss Confederation of the British North American colonies, including the framework for a new country and its government. John A. Macdonald, joint-premier of the province of Canada, is a driving force behind implementing the decisions made at that conference and at the Québec conference two months later. Following another conference held in London from December 1866 to February 1867, the British North America Act is enacted by British parliament on March 29, 1867, paving the way for the Confederation of Canada.

The 1860s

Birth of a Nation
and a Rebellion

1867

- July 1: The British colonies of Canada, Nova Scotia and New Brunswick unite to form the Dominion of Canada under the British North America Act (BNA), then divide to form four provinces: Ontario, Québec, Nova Scotia and New Brunswick.

- Ottawa, Ontario, is named the capital city of Canada.

- Sir John A. Macdonald becomes the first prime minister of Canada.

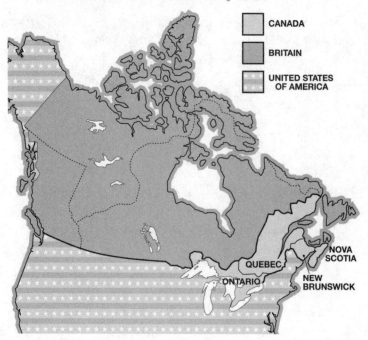

DOMINION OF CANADA, 1867

CANADA

BRITAIN

UNITED STATES OF AMERICA

QUEBEC

ONTARIO

NOVA SCOTIA

NEW BRUNSWICK

1868

- The Dominion Police is a small force established to guard the parliament buildings following the assassination of Thomas D'Arcy McGee, one of the Fathers of Confederation. The force remained active until 1920, when it merged with the Royal North-West Mounted Police to form the Royal Canadian Mounted Police.

- The Federal Militia Act, sponsored by George-Etienne Cartier, provides Canada with its own local army. Volunteers became the backbone of Canada's militia.

- The Canadian Red Ensign becomes Canada's unofficial national flag.

1869

- Canada agrees to purchase Rupert's Land and the North-Western Territory from the Hudson's Bay Company to form the North-West Territories, which was one-third of the current land area of Canada.

- The Red River Rebellion begins when people in the Red River Colony, mostly French-speaking Metis, form a provisional government led by Louis Riel to negotiate terms for entering Confederation.

- Timothy Eaton opens his first store in Toronto. Eaton's grew to become a retail giant in Canada before its eventual demise in 1999.

The 1870s

Growth of a Nation, the North-West Mounted Police and Building a Railway

1870

- The Red River Rebellion ends with the passing of the Manitoba Act on May 12, which guarantees Metis land claims and French-language rights and schools, with Canada reserving the right to all unclaimed lands and natural resources.

- Manitoba officially becomes Canada's fifth province on July 15.

1871

- The first census puts the Canadian population at 3,737,257 people.

- The federal government begins signing a series of treaties with western First Nations for the "taking up" of land, paving the way for immigration and settlement of the prairies.

- On July 20, British Columbia becomes Canada's sixth province. Feeling isolated on the west coast from the rest of Canada, BC's condition for joining Confederation is a transcontinental railway, promised by Prime Minister Macdonald.

1872

- The government passes legislation to legalize labour unions, but outlaw strikes and picketing.

- Parliament also passes the Dominion Lands Act, which encourages western settlement by providing a quarter-section of arable land to a homesteader for a small fee. The settler must also build a residence and cultivate the land.

- John A. Macdonald and his Conservatives are reelected in the federal election on October 12.

1873

- The North-West Mounted Police (NWMP) is formed on May 23 to police and assert sovereignty over the North-West Territories.

- The Cypress Hills Massacre of June 1, during which 30 or more Natives died in a conflict involving wolf hunters, whisky traders and a camp of Assiniboine people in the region of what is now Battle Creek, Saskatchewan, increases the urgency for recruitment and deployment of the newly formed NWMP.

- On July 1, Prince Edward Island becomes the seventh Canadian province. Financially bankrupt, PEI joined Confederation in exchange for Canada taking on its debt. Canada also pledged a ferry connection to the island and promised to buy back large tracts of land from absentee owners.

- The Pacific Scandal: News breaks in April that Macdonald and several of his fellow Conservatives had accepted contributions to their reelection campaign the previous fall in exchange for the contract to build the railway across the country. Evidence of wrongdoing mounts over the coming months, and by November, Macdonald is forced to resign as prime minister. Alexander Mackenzie and his Liberal Party take over.

1874

- Alexander Mackenzie defeats John A. Macdonald in a federal election on January 22, proving the people of Canada are not yet ready to forgive the Pacific Scandal.

- The Great March West begins on July 8 when 300 officers and men of the North-West Mounted Police (NWMP) set out from Dufferin, Manitoba, on a difficult two-month march across the prairies. While some men head north to set up a post in Fort Edmonton, most of the men eventually arrive at Fort Whoop-Up (today Lethbridge, Alberta), where they successfully clear out the whisky trade and establish order in the area. In October, the NWMP set up their base of operations at Fort Macleod.

1875

- Tensions between Catholic and Protestant New Brunswickers over the Common Schools Act of 1871 erupt in violence on January 26, claiming the lives of two men. The result is compromise on both sides.

- On April 5, the Supreme Court of Canada is founded to standardize Canadian law and interpret the constitution. People seeking a high-court legal decision are no longer required to travel to London, England, to have their cases heard.

- On June 1, construction begins on the Thunder Bay section of the transcontinental railway, linking Lake Superior to Winnipeg.

1876

• The Intercolonial Railway, linking Nova Scotia, New Brunswick, Québec and Ontario, is complete and open for business on July 1. Sandford Fleming, the future father of international standard time, was the man at the helm of the project.

• On August 10, Alexander Graham Bell makes the first long distance telephone call from his home in Brantford, Ontario, to a boot shop in Paris, Ontario.

• The Indian Act is passed by parliament, setting up the reserve land system for First Nations in Canada. The act guarantees irrevocable homelands by law and defines a "status" Indian. The controversial act is still in effect today, with several amendments.

1877

- The University of Manitoba, the oldest university in western Canada, is founded on February 28.

- The Great Fire of Saint John, New Brunswick, destroys over 1600 structures in just over nine hours on June 20. At least 18 people are killed, and many more are injured.

- James Cockshutt founds the Brantford Plow Works. Over the next several years, his business grows to become a major player in the tractor industry.

1878

- John A. Macdonald defeats Alexander Mackenzie in the federal election September 17, and he is officially sworn in as prime minister for a second time one month later.

- The first bull and cow moose are released in Newfoundland. Another introduction of four moose will take place in 1904. Today there are approximately 120,000 moose on the island, making it the area with the highest concentration of moose in the country.

- Anti-Chinese sentiment in British Columbia reaches a new high when the provincial government excludes Chinese workers from public works projects and introduces the Chinese Tax Act, which requires Chinese residents over age 12 to pay a $10 licence fee every three months. The next year, the act is declared unconstitutional and struck down.

1879

- Prime Minister Macdonald puts his National Policy into practice, raising tariffs on imported goods to protect Canadian manufacturers from American competition. Over time, the National Policy is broadened to include other Conservative government projects including building the transcontinental railway, subsidizing steamship service, developing ports and harbours and expanding western settlement.

- Parliament declares a day of Thanksgiving on November 6. It is a national rather than a religious holiday. The holiday moves around over the coming years until 1957, when Parliament proclaims the second Monday in October to be Canada's Thanksgiving Day.

The 1880s

O Canada, Canadian Pacific Railway and another Rebellion

1880

- "O Canada" ("*Chant national*") is first performed in Québec City on June 24. Several English versions follow, but the French lyrics remain unaltered to this day.

- Emily Stowe, Canada's first woman doctor, is finally granted a licence to practice medicine in Ontario, though she completed her training in 1867 in the U.S. and had been practicing in Toronto ever since.

- The Royal Canadian Academy of Arts is founded under the patronage of the Governor General, the Marquess of Lorne. Among the charter members are Canada's premier painters, sculptors, architects and designers.

1881

- The Canadian Pacific Railway (CPR) is incorporated on February 16. The company is given generous funding and land grants to complete the ambitious railway building project that Prime Minister Macdonald considered a national imperative. CPR president George Stephen hires W.C. Van Horne to oversee construction.

- The April 4 census puts the Canadian population at 4,381,256 people.

- The first grain elevator built to CPR specifications is constructed at Gretna, Manitoba. By 1933, grain elevators number as many as 5758 and dominate the prairie landscape. Today, fewer than 400 remain.

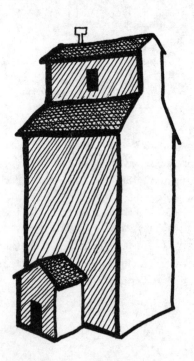

1882

- On May 17, provisional districts are created in the southern portion of the North-West Territories between Manitoba and British Columbia: Saskatchewan, Assiniboia, Alberta and Athabasca.

- John A. Macdonald's Conservatives win another majority government in the federal election on June 20.

- The North-West Mounted Police moves its headquarters from Fort Macleod to Regina, North-West Territories (now Saskatchewan).

- The Royal Society of Canada is founded by the Governor General, the Marquess of Lorne, and leading scholars of the day. It is an organization for the promotion of learning and research and remains important today.

1883

- Nickel-copper ore is discovered at Sudbury, Ontario, during construction of the Canadian Pacific Railway. Within a few years, Sudbury is Canada's first major mining camp.

- A new Militia Act adds permanent staff for militia schools, which become the nucleus of a professional force.

- Augusta Stowe-Gullen, daughter of Dr. Emily Stowe, is the first woman to graduate from a Canadian medical school.

- On November 18, North American railways adopt standardized time and a system of hour-wide time zones. Canada's Sir Sandford Fleming was behind initial efforts to create standard time zones and developed the global system used today.

1884

- The Railway Relief Act is passed to provide the CPR with additional millions in loans to cover high construction costs.

- Canadians are called on to aid a British expedition to the Sudan to rescue British soldiers and Egyptian garrisons cut off by a Muslim uprising. The British commander believed Canadian "voyageurs" could offer the expertise needed to navigate the Nile. Nearly 400 volunteers went and proved themselves admirably, though the mission itself was unsuccessful.

- Eaton's produces its first mail-order catalogue. Within a decade, Eaton's has largely cornered the mail-order business in Canada, targeting rural customers with limited access to its stores.

1885

- North-West Rebellion: Beginning in March and over by July, the rebellion is a violent insurgency against the government fought mainly by Metis and their First Nations allies in what is now Sasakatchewan. Led by Louis Riel, they were fighting for land rights and their way of life. Riel is convicted of treason and hanged at Regina on November 16.

- On November 7, the last spike of the Canadian Pacific Railway is driven in at Craigellachie, British Columbia, by CPR director Donald Smith.

- Banff National Park is established. It is Canada's first and most visited national park.

- The Chinese Immigration Act levies a head tax on Chinese immigrants. This legislation is the first in Canadian history to exclude immigrants based on ethnicity.

1886

- On April 6, Vancouver is incorporated as a city, and its citizens vote in real estate salesman Malcolm A. MacLean as mayor. Real estate salesmen are still running the show in Vancouver.

- Only two months later, on June 13, the Great Vancouver Fire devastates the new city. Mortality is high and property damage is as high as $1.3 million.

1887

- John A. Macdonald's Conservatives win a third consecutive majority in the federal election on February 22.

- A coal mine explosion near Nanaimo, British Columbia, on May 3 kills 148 miners. It is BC's worst coal mining disaster.

- The first interprovincial premiers' conference, organized by Québec premier Honore Mercier, is held at Québec City in October. There the premiers agree to work together to maintain some provincial autonomy to counter Macdonald's ideal of centralism.

- *Saturday Night*, Canada's oldest general interest magazine, begins as a weekly broadsheet newspaper in Toronto on December 3 and ends publication in November 2005.

1888

- The North-West Territories holds its first general election on June 20, electing 22 members to its legislative assembly. All are independents; the territory has no political parties.

- During September and October, an Ontario soccer team tours Great Britain and startles their hosts by beating most of the opposing teams, earning praise from the English papers.

1889

- On September 19, a rock slide in Québec City kills more than 40 people. It is bad, but could have been worse: several families who lived on the street the slide destroyed were not home at the time.

- Parliament passes an anti-combines law to protect competition in the marketplace, but it is flawed in that it leaves room for interpretation. The rich find a way to get richer.

The 1890s

The Stanley Cup, Manitoba Schools and the Klondike Gold Rush

1890

- The first wave of Dutch immigration to Canada begins and lasts until 1914. The majority of Dutch immigrants were drawn to the rich farmland of the prairies. Two more waves will occur, one from 1923 to 1930, and another following World War II, from 1947 to the late 1960s.

- Isaac Shupe of Newmarket, Ontario, provides some relief from tedium with his time-saving invention of an automatic soap dispenser for clothes washing plungers.

1891

- An explosion at a mine near Springhill, Nova Scotia, on February 21 kills 125 workers. It is unfortunately only the first of three mining disasters to devastate the town.

- On March 5, Macdonald wins a fourth consecutive federal election on the platform of continued protectionism against the United States.

- The April 6 census puts the Canadian population at 4,932,206 people.

- On June 6, Prime Minister Sir John A. Macdonald, Canada's first prime minister and the most prominent figure in Canadian public service, dies of a stroke. He is succeeded in office by John Abbott.

- The Calgary and Edmonton Railway opens on December 10, connecting Edmonton to the national rail network.

1892

- On March 18, Governor General Lord Stanley announces that he will donate a silver cup to be awarded to Canada's top hockey team each year. Originally called the Dominion Hockey Challenge Cup, it was first awarded to the Montréal Amateur Athletic Association following the 1892–1893 season. We now know it as the Stanley Cup, awarded to the top National Hockey League team since 1926.

- The Criminal Code of Canada is enacted on July 9 under the direction of Justice Minister John Thompson. It has never been fundamentally revised, but it has been amended many times over the years to keep up with technological, social and economic changes in society.

- John Thompson becomes prime minister on December 5 after John Abbott resigns.

1893

- Algonquin Provincial Park is established in Ontario on May 27. It is the first provincial park in Canada.

- The National Council of Women of Canada (NCWC) meets for the first time on October 27 in Toronto. It is affiliated with the International Council of Women (ICW), founded in the U.S. in 1888. The NCWC's first president is Lady Aberdeen, the wife of Canada's Governor General. The organization unites various women's groups across the country.

1894

- Labour Day is officially observed for the first time on September 3. Although parades and rallies in support of organized labour had been held in Canada annually since 1872, it wasn't until July 23, 1894, that Prime Minister Thompson declared a national holiday to be celebrated every year on the first Monday in September.

- On December 10, two of Newfoundland and Labrador's three banks crash, the result of years of mismanagement. The day becomes known as Black Monday. Following the crash, the colony adopted the Canadian currency.

- John Thompson dies on December 12 while in London, England, shortly after being made a member of the Privy Council by Queen Victoria. He is succeeded in office by Mackenzie Bowell on December 21.

- Margaret Marshall Saunders, from Nova Scotia, wins the American Humane Society's writers' competition with a novel about an abused dog called *Beautiful Joe*. The book becomes a bestseller, eventually translated into 14 languages and the first Canadian book to sell more than one million copies.

1895

- Maria Grant is the first woman in Canada to be elected to any political office when she is elected to Victoria, British Columbia's school board in March. She will serve six years on the board.

- On October 2, additional provisional districts are created in the North-West Territories: Ungava, Mackenzie, Franklin and the gold-producing Yukon.

1896

- On April 27, Mackenzie Bowell resigns as prime minister owing to cabinet infighting. He is replaced by Charles Tupper on May 1.

- Wilfrid Laurier and his Liberal Party win a majority in the federal election on June 23. Laurier is officially sworn in as prime minister on July 11.

- Gold is discovered in a tributary of the Yukon River in mid-August.

• Manitoba Schools Question: The question of French-speaking
Catholic rights in Manitoba, and in their schools in particular,
had been an issue since Manitoba joined Confederation. Back
in 1870, the population was even between French Catholics
and English Protestants, but over the years the demographics
changed with the arrival of more settlers, most of them British.
In 1890, the Protestant-controlled provincial government of
Thomas Greenway abolished separate schools, required all residents to pay school taxes and made English the sole language
of law and government. French-speaking Manitobans were furi-
ous, and sympathy for their plight spread to engulf the entire
country. In January 1896, the federal government led by
Mackenzie Bowell introduces a remedial bill to restore the
lost rights of Manitoba Francophones, but it is defeated, as
is his government over the issue. On November 16, Wilfrid
Laurier's government introduces a compromise solution that
does not reverse the 1890 legislation but does restore some
French Catholic rights. The crisis is over.

1897

- Klondike Gold Rush: When word of the Yukon gold discovery gets out, a mad rush for riches begins. With so much traffic headed for the Klondike, the Canadian government sends in the North-West Mounted Police to control the flow of people and collect a royalty from the gold. The NWMP set up a checkpoint at the Chilkoot Pass and require each miner to carry with him enough supplies to survive for a year. This "proving up" is unpopular but saves many lives. Although a lucky few did strike it rich, many thousands more left disappointed.

- The Crowsnest Pass Agreement of September 6 between CPR and the Canadian government gives the CPR a subsidy to extend the railway through the Crowsnest Pass in exchange for lowering its freight rates for prairie farmers to get their grain to markets. Called the "Crow rate," it remains in effect in varying forms until 1994.

- The first Canadian movies are produced by Manitoba farmer James Freer. Collectively entitled *Ten Years in Manitoba*, they depict life on the prairies.

1898

- On June 13, with the gold rush in full swing, Yukon becomes a separate territory with Dawson City as its capital. The capital is moved to Whitehorse in 1953.

- The federal government holds a plebicite on September 29 on the issue of the prohibition of alcohol. Only 44 percent of the electorate voted: 51 percent yes and 49 percent no. Prime Minister Laurier decides the result is too close to warrant passing a law and instead leaves it the the provinces to make their own decisions regarding alcohol.

1899

- William Mackenzie and Donald Mann form the Canadian Northern Railway (CNoR) to expand railway lines in the west. Many prairie cities and towns owe their existence to the CNoR.

- The Boer War begins in October, with Britain declaring war against the Boers of South Africa. Canadian opinion is divided over whether to get involved; Prime Minister Laurier eventually authorizes a volunteer force. It is the first time Canada sends soldiers overseas and into battle wearing Canadian uniforms.

The 1900s

National Pride, New Provinces and the Grey Cup

1900

- Canadian troops are responsible for the first significant British victory of the Boer War during the Battle of Paardeberg in February. It is a point of national pride.

- Although Canada does not send an official team, Canadian middle-distance runner George Orton accompanies the American team to the Summer Olympics in Paris and wins two medals: a gold and a bronze.

- Wilfrid Laurier's Liberals win a second consecutive majority in the federal election on November 7.

1901

- Queen Victoria dies on January 22. After 63 years on the throne, her death is the end of an era.

- The March 31 census puts the Canadian population at 5,418,663 people.

- Although Victoria Day, the queen's birthday, has been celebrated for years in Canada, May 24 is officially declared a national holiday. In 1952, Victoria Day is fixed as the first Monday before May 25. Today, it marks the unofficial start to the summer season.

- On December 12, Italian inventor Guglielmo Marconi and his assistant, George Kemp, ensconced in a small hut on a Newfoundland cliff top, hear three dots sent from a transmitter in England. It is the first transatlantic radio signal.

1902

- The Boer War ends on May 31. Canadian troops had distinguished themselves well. Four Canadians received the Victoria Cross; 270 Canadians lost their lives.

- Immigration to Canada, a large portion of which is from Great Britain, kicks into high gear and continues until the beginning of World War I in 1914.

1903

- On April 29 at 4:10 AM, in 90 seconds, 82 million tonnes
  of rock from Turtle Mountain suddenly slides down into the
  Crowsnest Valley in what is now the southwestern corner of
  Alberta. The slide buries the eastern outskirts of the town
  of Frank, as well as a two-kilometre stretch of railway and
  a coalmine entrance. The number of dead is estimated to be
  at least 70; likely more. Frank Slide remains Canada's deadliest
  rock slide.

• Silver is discovered by railway workers in northern Ontario on August 7. By 1905, the town of Cobalt had sprung up as the hub of the silver rush. By the 1930s, most of the mines were closed.

• The Alaska boundary dispute between Canada and the U.S. for the Alaskan panhandle is finally settled on October 20 by an international tribunal made up of three Americans, two Canadians and one Brit, the Lord Chief Justice of England, Lord Alverstone. As expected, the Americans and Canadians vote for their respective countries' claims. In what is seen as a betrayal, Alverstone sides with the American claim, leading to a strong wave of anti-British sentiment in Canada.

1904

- A new Militia Act sets up a Militia Council of civilians and military officials, and it doubles the permanent force to 4000 to provide a garrison for Halifax to replace departing British troops.

- Canada sends its first official team to the Summer Olympics in St. Louis. The Canadian athletes come home with four gold medals and one silver.

- On August 14, the Ford Motor Company of Canada is founded in Walkerville, Ontario, now part of Windsor.

- Wilfrid Laurier and his Liberal Party win a third consecutive majority in the federal election on November 3.

1905

- On August 25, Norwegian explorer Roald Amundsen becomes the first to successfully navigate a ship through the Northwest Passage.

- On September 1, Alberta and Saskatchewan enter Confederation as Canada's eighth and ninth provinces. Alberta combines the former North-West Territories districts of Alberta and Athabasca, and Saskatchewan combines the districts of Saskatchewan and Assiniboia. Local leaders wanted provincial status as a way to control their own affairs.

1906

- A new Immigration Act introduces a more restrictive immigration policy than previously existed. It expands the categories of prohibited immigrants—such as the sick, destitute and criminal—formalizes a deportation process and gives the government the power to make arbitrary decisions on admission.

- Canadian radio inventor Reginald Fessenden achieves the first two-way voice transmission by radio, between Scotland and Massachusetts. On Christmas Eve, he makes the first public radio broadcast of music and voice to ships on the Atlantic.

1907

- The McLaughlin Car Company begins manufacturing Buicks in Oshawa, Ontario. In 1915, McLaughlin acquires Chevrolet Canada, and in 1918, the company will become General Motors of Canada.

- Despite discriminatory legislation already limiting the rights of Asians in British Columbia, anti-Asian sentiment explodes into riots in Vancouver from September 7 to 9 targeting Chinese, Japanese and South Asians. No one is killed, but damage is extensive.

1908

• The Royal Canadian Mint opens on January 2, producing the first made-in-Canada coins.

• *Anne of Green Gables*, by L.M. Montgomery, is first published in April. Anne remains Prince Edward Island's most popular heroine, even today. The series of Anne books has been translated into 15 languages.

• Canadians win three gold, three silver and nine bronze medals at the Summer Olympics in London.

• Wilfred Laurier's Liberals win a fourth consecutive majority in the federal election on October 26.

• P.L. Robertson invents the square-headed screw and screwdriver and establishes a manufacturing plant in Milton, Ontario.

1909

- The Boundary Waters Treaty is signed on January 11 between Canada and the United States to prevent and solve disputes regarding water use along the international boundary. It also prohibits the diversion of waters without approval by the International Joint Commission, the first permanent joint organization between the two countries.

- On February 23, J.A.D. McCurdy makes the first powered flight in the British Empire from Baddeck Bay, Nova Scotia. Alexander Graham Bell was the leader of the team that engineered the aircraft called the Silver Dart.

- December 4 is a big day for Canadian sports. The Grey Cup, donated to Canadian football by Governor General Earl Grey, is first awarded to a team from the University of Toronto. Also on this day, the Montréal Canadiens are founded as a team in the National Hockey Association (NHA). After the NHA folds, the team is a founding member of the National Hockey League (NHL) in 1917. The Canadiens are Canada's most successful team, having won 24 Stanley Cups to date.

The 1910s

Parks Canada, an Arctic Expedition, World War I and Women's Suffrage

1910

- The Naval Service Bill, introduced on January 10 and passed by Laurier's majority government on May 4, creates the Department of the Naval Service, later renamed the Royal Canadian Navy. The act highlights the deep divisions in Canada between pro- and anti-imperialists, one side wanting to support Britain's international interests and the other wanting to stay out of it. By fall, Canada had purchased two ships: one for the Pacific coast at Esquimault and one for the Atlantic at Halifax.

- It is a disastrous year for Canadians across the country. On January 21, a train wreck near Sudbury, Ontario, kills more than 40 people. On March 4, an avalanche in Rogers Pass, British Columbia, kills at least 58 people. And on December 9, a coal mine explosion at Bellevue, Alberta, kills at least 30 people.

1911

- The Dominion Parks Branch, later Parks Canada, is formed on May 19 to administer Canada's national parks. Today, Parks Canada manages more than 40 national parks and national park reserves.

- The June 1 census puts the Canadian population at 7,221,662 people.

- Robert Borden and his Conservative Party win a majority in the federal election on September 21. Borden is officially sworn in as prime minister on October 10. His campaign focused on the controversy of the Naval Service Bill to defeat Laurier.

- Marquis wheat wins an award for the best wheat variety in Canada. Developed by Dr. Charles Saunders, Marquis wheat greatly increased wheat production on the prairies and grew Canada into the world's largest exporter of wheat.

1912

- The *Titanic* hits an iceburg off the coast of Newfoundland on April 14, and by the next morning, the ship is sunk. Three Halifax-based crews are pressed into service to gather the dead. Some 150 souls are laid to rest in three Halifax cemeteries.

- Canada wins three gold, two silver and two bronze medals at the Stockholm Olympics. George Hodgson is Canada's first double gold medalist, in swimming.

- The first Calgary Stampede rodeo is held on September 2. Today, the "Greatest Outdoor Show on Earth" attracts hundreds of thousands of visitors to Calgary each July.

1913

- The Canadian Arctic Expedition begins in June, commanded by Vilhjalmur Stefansson. It is Canada's largest, most expensive and scientifically advanced venture to date, and it is financed by the government. Over the next five years, through many hardships, the expedition asserts Canada's sovereignty in the North, discovers new islands and redraws the map, and collects scientific data.

- Immigration to Canada reaches its peak; more than 400,000 people arrive to begin new lives.

- The Laura Secord Candy Store opens in Toronto. Frank P. O'Connor named his store after the Canadian heroine of the War of 1812. Today, Laura Secord products are sold across Canada.

1914

- On May 14, oil and gas are discovered at Turner Valley, Alberta. The discovery helps start the oil and gas industry in the province.

- A coal mine explosion at Hillcrest, Alberta, on June 19 kills 189 miners. It is Canada's worst mining disaster.

- World War I begins on August 4. Canada, as part of the British Empire, is pulled into the war alongside Britain. On October 3, 33,000 volunteer troops depart for Europe.

- The War Measures Act is passed on August 14 and is in effect until 1920. It gives the government broad powers to maintain security and order, including the suspension of civil liberties. Its use was and remains controversial.

1915

- On January 23, the Canadian Northern Railway completes its line to Vancouver.

- The Second Battle of Ypres, fought April 22–May 25, is the first major battle for Canadian forces, during which they suffer the first chemical weapons attack of the war. They make rudimentary gas masks of urine-soaked rags and manage to hold their ground.

- On May 3, John McCrae writes "In Flanders Fields." First published later that year in *Punch* magazine, a British weekly, the poem is now read by millions worldwide every Remembrance Day.

1916

- On February 3, the Centre Block of the Parliament Buildings in Ottawa burns down. Only the Parliamentary Library survives. Reconstruction begins a few months later.

- Women in three provinces win the right to vote: in Manitoba on January 28; in Saskatchewan on March 14; and in Alberta on April 19. Emily Murphy becomes the first female magistrate in Canada.

- The Battle of the Somme, fought from July 1 to November 18, claims more than 24,000 Canadians and Newfoundlanders—among almost 1.2 million men in total. The cost is high for very little gain.

- On July 29, a fire begins in the bush around Matheson, Ontario. Over the next few days, it will destroy thousands of hectares and kill more than 200 people. It remains Canada's deadliest forest fire.

- The National Research Council (NRC) of Canada is founded. It is Canada's premier organization for scientific research and development. The NRC is responsible for helping to develop the motorized wheelchair, aviation advances including radar, bomb detection equipment, anti-counterfeit devices, computer animation, life-saving medical vaccines and the famous Canadarm used by NASA.

1917

- Women in two more provinces win the right to vote: in British Columbia on April 5; and in Ontario on April 12. Louise McKinney is elected to the Alberta legislature on June 7, the first woman elected to a legislature in Canada and in the British Empire.

- At the Battle of Vimy Ridge, fought April 9–12, four Canadian divisions fight together for the first time and succeed in capturing the ridge from the Germans. It is a moment of Canadian pride, but the cost is high; more than 10,500 Canadians are killed or wounded.

- By now, volunteers for the war effort have slowed to a trickle, and the high numbers of casualties in Europe had taken their toll. Prime Minister Borden believes conscription is the answer. The Military Service Act becomes law on August 29 and sets off a conscription crisis, dividing Canada largely along English-speaking supporters and French-speaking opposers.

- On September 20, Borden's government introduces a "temporary" income tax, with lower incomes exempt and higher incomes taxed as much as 25 percent. Income tax survives the war, and by 1939, it is generating almost one-third of federal government revenue.

- During fall's muddy, bloody Battle of Passchendaele, Canada suffers 15,600 casualties—yet another high cost to pay for very little gain.

- The National Hockey League is formed on November 26 with four teams: the Montréal Canadiens, Montréal Wanderers, Ottawa Senators and Toronto Arenas.

- On December 6, the north end of Halifax is destroyed by an explosion and subsequent tsunami after two ships collide in the harbour, one of them loaded with munitions. Nearly 2000 people are killed, 9000 are wounded and more than 25,000 are left homeless. Railway dispacher Vincent Coleman is a hero for stopping an incoming passenger train at the cost of his own life.

- The federal election, scheduled for December 17, is basically about conscription. Borden stacks the vote in his favour by passing the Military Voters Act, which gives all Canadian soldiers the right to vote even if they are under age or British-born, and the Wartime Elections Act, which gives women serving in the Canadian Army Medical Corps and close female relatives of servicemen the right to vote in the federal election, as well as removing the right to vote from immigrants from enemy nations. Borden wins a second majority, defeating Laurier's Liberals.

1918

- Women in Nova Scotia win the right to vote on April 26. On May 24, female citizens of Canada are granted the right to vote in federal elections. New Brunswick women get the vote the next year, Prince Edward Island women in 1922, and women in Newfoundland in 1925. Québec women must wait until 1940.

- On November 11, World War I comes to an end. It cost 61,000 Canadian lives, and many thousands more return home injured in body and mind.

1919

- The Winnipeg General Strike begins on May 15 when 30,000 public and private workers in that city walk off the job, holding out for better wages and working conditions. City employers refuse to negotiate. The federal government takes the side of the employers. On June 17, police arrest 10 strike leaders. On June 21, a charge of Royal North-West Mounted Police into a crowd of demonstrators leads to 30 casualties, including one death, and becomes known as Bloody Saturday. Defeated, the strike ends four days later on June 25.

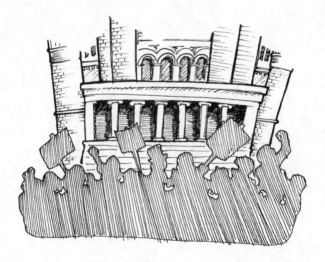

- Canadian National Railways (CNR) is incorporated on June 6 as an amalgamation of several struggling railway companies, including Canadian Northern and Grand Trunk.

- The Treaty of Versailles officially ends World War I on June 28. Canada had its own representation at the negotiations and is a signatory on the treaty, though only as part of the British Empire. Canada does win separate membership in the League of Nations, an organization founded as a result of the treaty.

The 1920s

The Royal Canadian Mounted Police, Banting and Best, the King-Byng Affair and the Persons Case

1920

- The Royal Canadian Mounted Police (RCMP) is formed on February 1 by a merger of the Royal North-West Mounted Police and the Dominion Police.

- The Group of Seven forms and holds their first exibition at the Art Gallery of Toronto in May. The influence of the group on Canadian art remains to this day.

- Robert Borden retires from Canadian politics, and Arthur Meighen is appointed prime minister on July 10.

- Ice hockey is an Olympic sport for the first time, at the Antwerp Summer Games. Canada wins gold!

1921

- The *Bluenose* is launched at Lunenburg, Nova Scotia, on March 26. It is a fishing vessel also designed to race on the open ocean. The image of Canada's most famous ship first appears on the Canadian dime in 1937 and remains there to this day.

- The June 1 census puts the Canadian population at 8,800,249 people.

- William Lyon Mackenzie King's Liberal Party wins the federal election on December 6, defeating Arthur Meighen's Conservatives. Agnes Macphail of Ontario runs in the election for the Progressive Party and is the first woman elected to the House of Commons.

- Dr. Frederick Banting takes his idea of how to isolate insulin for the treatment of diabetes to the University of Toronto, and on May 17, under the direction of J.J.R. Macleod, Banting and a student assistant, Charles Best, begin their experiments. James Bertram Collip, a biochemist, joins the team in December. A breakthrough in January 1922 leads to a public announcement in May at a conference in Washington, D.C., about the discovery of insulin. Banting and Macleod will win the Nobel Prize for their efforts in 1923. They share the prize with Best and Collip.

1922

- Canada's new coat of arms, bestowed the previous year, is authorized to be placed on the Canadian Red Ensign on April 26.

- In what will become known as the Chanak Affair, Prime Minister King declines to send soldiers to aid British troops in Turkey without first putting the matter to Parliament. It is another step toward independence from Britain.

1923

- Canada signs the Halibut Treaty, an agreement on fishing rights, with the United States on March 2. It is the first international treaty that Canada signs separate from Britain.

- On July 1, the Chinese Immigration Act is passed, effectively banning Chinese immigrants for the next 24 years, with very few exceptions. Only the Chinese were ever singled out for immigration restrictions solely on the basis of race.

- Marijuana is criminalized in Canada as part of Prime Minister King's Act to Prohibit the Improper Use of Opium and other Drugs.

1924

- At the first Winter Olympics in Chamonix, France, Canada wins gold in ice hockey.

- The Royal Canadian Air Force is formed on April 1. During World War I, Canadian pilots had flown under Britain's Royal Air Force.

1925

- Chrysler Canada is incorporated in Windsor, Ontario, on June 17, and production is soon booming.

- On June 23, a joint Canadian-American expedition is the first to reach the summit of Mount Logan, the highest mountain in Canada.

- In August, Edward (Ted) Rogers Sr. perfects and launches a batteryless radio and revolutionizes the home radio industry worldwide.

- The federal election on October 29 pits William Lyon Mackenzie King's Liberals against Arthur Meighen's Conservatives, with the Progressive Party as the wildcard. Meighen wins the election, but King refuses to step down, instead partnering with the Progressives to form a fragile alliance. It is a precarious situation for the government.

1926

- The King-Byng Affair dominates politics. In June, King loses the support of the Progressives and is faced with a no-confidence vote. He asks Governor General Byng to dissolve Parliament and call an election; Byng refuses. King resigns his seat, and Meighen is appointed prime minister on June 29. However, Meighen is unsuccessful in gaining the confidence of the House of Commons. Byng grants a dissolution of Parliament, and an election is called for September 14. This time King wins; he is prime minister once again.

- The Balfour Report, released in November, declares that Britain and its Dominions, including Canada, are equal, but they remain united with Britain and the other Dominions through the Commonwealth.

- A.A. Milne's *Winnie-the-Pooh* is published in London, a children's book inspired by a Canadian black bear.

1927

- Conn Smythe purchases the Toronto franchise of the NHL in February and renames the team the Toronto Maple Leafs.

- After a years-long dispute, on March 1, the boundary between Labrador and Québec is finally settled in its present location.

- Parliament enacts the first old-age pension on May 28, to be jointly financed by federal and provincial governments but administered by the provinces.

- In November, Emily Carr is invited to exhibit her art at the National Gallery of Canada and becomes nationally known.

1928

- At the Winter Olympics in St. Moritz, Switzerland, Canada wins hockey gold. The team was coached by Conn Smythe.

- Canadians do well at the Summer Olympics in Amsterdam, Netherlands. These games are the first to include women's track-and-field events; the Canadian women's team wins two gold, a silver and a bronze medal.

- On August 25, a BC Airways plane crashes into Puget Sound, killing seven people. It is Canada's first commercial air disaster.

1929

- On October 18, women are officially declared "persons" under the law. It is the culmination of a court battle begun in 1927 by the Famous Five: Henrietta Muir Edwards, Nellie McClung, Louise McKinney, Emily Murphy and Irene Parlby. When the Supreme Court of Canada ruled against them in 1928, they took their Persons Case to the Privy Council of England, which reversed the Supreme Court's decision. Women are now able to hold any political office.

- The U.S. stock market crashes on October 29, setting off the Great Depression worldwide. Canada will be especially hard hit.

The 1930s

Depression, Quintland
and the CBC

1930

- On February 15, Cairine Wilson is the first woman appointed to the Senate.

- R.B. Bennett's Conservatives win the federal election on July 28, defeating William Lyon Mackenzie King's Liberals. During his campaign, Bennett promised Canadians he would aggressively combat the Great Depression. He is sworn in as prime minister on August 7.

1931

- The June 1 census puts the Canadian population at 10,376,379 people.

- On December 11, the Statute of Westminster makes law the findings of Balfour Report of 1926: that Canada has full legislative independence in both domestic and foreign affairs.

1932

- Canada does well at the Lake Placid Winter Olympics in February, including winning gold in hockey.

- On May 26, the Canadian Radio Broadcasting Commission (CRBC) is formed as Canada's first public broadcaster. It is the forerunner to the Canadian Broadcasting Corporation (CBC).

- The Ottawa Agreements between Canada and Britain result in preferential rates to trade with Britain over other countries, including the United States.

- Canada wins 15 medals at the Los Angeles Summer Olympics.

1933

- The Great Depression is at its height. Almost one-third of Canada's workforce is unemployed. The prairie provinces have it the worst; years of drought, grasshopper plagues and hail storms lead to crop failures. Many Canadians blame Prime Minister Bennett for their plight.

- Toronto-born cartoonist Joe Shuster and Cleveland, Ohio, writer Jerry Siegel create Superman, the mighty comic book hero able to leap tall buildings in a single bound.

1934

- The Dionne quintuplets—Annette, Emilie, Yvonne, Cecile and Marie—are born on May 28. They are the world's first quintuplets to survive infancy. The Ontario government removes them from their parents' care and places them under their doctor's care in a specially built hospital that becomes known as Quintland. For nine years they are a lucrative tourist attraction. In 1998, the three surviving quints will be awarded $4 million in compensation.

- The Bank of Canada Act of July 3 leads to the creation of the Bank of Canada in March 1935. It is nationalized in 1938. The Bank of Canada is in charge of issuing paper currency and setting the national interest rate.

1935

- Frustrated unemployment relief camp workers in BC go on strike in April, and by June, having gotten nowhere, they decide to take their protest to Bennett himself. The On to Ottawa Trek begins June 3, with more than 1000 workers heading east. They are stopped in Regina, where they wait while eight trekkers go on to Ottawa. The June 22 meeting with Bennett does not go well, and they return to Regina. One last rally is called for July 1. RCMP move in on the crowd, provoking the Regina Riot. By the time it's all over, one Mountie is dead and many other Mounties, protesters and bystanders are injured.

- The Canadian Wheat Board is established on July 5 as the only buyer and seller of wheat and barley on the prairies to regulate the market.

- Canadians are unhappy with how Bennett has handled the Depression. In the federal election on October 14, King and his Liberals win a majority; King is sworn in for the third time October 23.

- The first entirely Canadian bush plane, designed and built in Montréal by R.B.C. Noorduyn, makes its first flight in November. The Noorduyn Norseman becomes a workhorse of the Canadian North.

1936

- On January 6, Barbara Hanley is elected mayor of Webbwood, Ontario, making her Canada's first woman mayor.

- At the Winter Olympics in February, Canada loses hockey gold to Great Britain, which sent a team stacked with British-born, Canadian players.

• The Canadian Broadcasting Corporation (CBC) is established on November 2 to take over from the struggling CRBC. Today, the CBC operates both radio and television networks in both English and French across the country, broadcasting primarily Canadian content.

1937

• Trans-Canada Airlines (TCA) is created on April 10 to provide air service to all regions of Canada. It is the forerunner to Air Canada.

• On June 14, the Happy Gang launches its radio variety show on the CBC. For 22 years it airs weekdays at noon, entertaining millions of Canadians.

• Québec native Joseph-Armand Bombardier's first snowmobile, the B7, hits the market. It seats seven people. His first single-seat Ski-Doo will be sold in 1959.

1938

- Franklin D. Roosevelt is the first U.S. president to pay an official visit to Canada. On August 18, he delivers a speech to a crowd in Kingston, Ontario, extolling the friendship and cooperation between our two countries.

- Elsie MacGill, Canada's first practicing woman engineer, is hired as the chief aeronautical engineer of Canadian Car and Foundry, where she will oversee production of Hawker Hurricane fighter planes during World War II.

1939

- Faced with an inevitable war and not wanting to run into the same problems encountered during World War I, the government establishes the Wartime Prices and Trade Board on September 3 to control wartime inflation.

- On September 10, Canada declares war on Germany. The first Canadian troops arrive in England in December.

The 1940s

World War II, Viola Desmond, Alberta Oil and Newfoundland

1940

- William Lyon Mackenzie King's Liberals win a second consecutive majority in the federal election on March 26.

- On June 10, Canada declares war on Italy.

- From July through October, the Battle of Britain is fought in the air. Hundreds of Canadians participate in helping Britain fend off Germany's Luftwaffe and its planned ground invasion.

- Unemployment insurance (now called employment insurance) is instituted on August 7 and is made compulsory for Canadian employers and employees to pay into.

1941

- The census puts the Canadian population at 11,506,655 people.

- Women in the military: Women want to serve, but it isn't until 1941 that they are able to enlist. In July, a women's auxiliary air force is created, and in August, an auxiliary army force is created. In February and March 1942, both women's forces are integrated into the regular air force and army, and by July, a women's division of the navy is created. Thousands of women volunteer over the course of the war, proving invaluable.

- On December 8, Canada declares war on Japan.

- The Battle of Hong Kong, December 8–25, is the first land battle of the war fought by Canadians. Inexperienced Canadian soldiers and their British counterparts are no match for the Japanese. Of the 2000 Canadian troops involved in the battle, 290 are killed outright and 264 will die in Japanese prisoner-of-war camps.

1942

- On April 27, the government holds a national referendum on conscription. More than 60 percent vote in favour of a draft, with only Québec voting overwhelmingly against it.

- In August, the Dieppe Raid—Operation Jubilee—is the Canadian army's first European battle of the war. It is another disaster. More than 900 Canadian soldiers are killed, with thousands more wounded and taken prisoner.

- Having departed two years earlier from Vancouver, Henry Larsen of the RCMP becomes the first to traverse Northwest Passage from west to east when he reaches Halifax in his ship, the *St. Roch*, on October 11.

- Japanese-Canadian internment: In February, the government orders the removal of Japanese Canadians from the BC coast. By September, nearly 22,000 men, women and children have been moved to internment camps in BC's interior or work camps farther east. Their property and belongings were seized and auctioned off, with the proceeds confiscated. At the end of the war, dispossessed Japanese are given the choice to move to Japan or relocate east of the Rockies. Not until 1988 do they receive an official apology and some compensation.

1943

- In August, Prime Minister King hosts Allied leaders Winston Churchill and Franklin Roosevelt at a war-planning conference in Québec City but doesn't directly take part.

- The Italian Campaign begins in July. Over the course of the next (nearly) two years, Canadian soldiers work their way from Sicily north, beating back the Germans. Almost 93,000 Canadians served in Italy, at a cost of more than 26,000 casualties.

1944

- The Battle of Normandy begins June 6 with the D-Day invasion and ends with the German defeat at Falais on August 21. It is the beginning of the end of the war, and Canada plays an important role. The Allies suffer 209,000 casualties, of which 18,700 are Canadian.

- The Family Allowance Act passes in Parliament on August 1 and begins the next year as Canada's first universal welfare program.

- Prime Minister King, faced with high casualties on the European front and the need for more manpower for the army, announces on November 22 that conscripts will be sent overseas, setting off a new Conscription Crisis and causing renewed tensions between Anglophones and Francophones.

1945

- In January, the city of Brantford, Ontario, becomes the first in Canada to add flouride to its municipal water supply in an 11-year test of the chemical's effectiveness. It seems to help reduce dental cavities in children, and other cities soon follow suit.

- On the war front, from February through April, Canada leads the push to free the Netherlands from German control. More than 7600 Canadians die fighting in the Netherlands. To this day, the Dutch fondly remember the Canadian soldiers who liberated their country. As well, the royal family of the Netherlands sent 100,000 tulip bulbs to Ottawa in appreciation for Canada sheltering Princess Juliana and her daughters during the Nazi occupation of World War II.

- On May 8, Germany surrenders to the Allies; it is VE Day, Victory in Europe.

- William Lyon Mackenzie King and his Liberals win a third consecutive majority in the federal election on June 11.

- On August 15, Japan surrenders to the Allies; it is VJ Day, Victory in Japan. World War II is officially over. Over the course of the war, nearly 44,000 Canadians lost their lives.

- On September 5, Igor Gouzenko, a Russian clerk working in Ottawa, defects from the Soviet Union and hands over Soviet secrets to the Canadian government. The "Gouzenko affair" illustrates the dangers of Soviet espionage.

- Canada is a founding member of the United Nations, formed October 24.

1946

- An earthquake hits Vancouver Island on June 23. It is a big one and causes a lot of damage, but thankfully only two deaths occur.

- On November 8, Viola Desmond takes a stand against racial discrimination at the Roseland Theatre in New Glasgow, Nova Scotia. Her legacy has since been honoured with a postage stamp in 2012 and a *Heritage Minute* in 2016, and she will be the first Canadian woman to appear on a Canadian banknote in 2018.

1947

- On January 1, the Canadian Citizenship Act comes into force. It is the first law to define people as Canadian, as opposed to British subjects.

- Oil is discovered at Leduc, Alberta, on February 13. By the end of the year, some 30 wells in the area are producing 3500 barrels of oil a day.

- The Chinese Immigration Act of 1923 is repealed on May 14, and Chinese (along with South Asian) Canadians are given the right to vote. Japanese Canadians will get the vote in 1949.

- Another Canadian bush plane, the de Havilland Beaver, makes its debut on August 16.

1948

- At the Winter Olympics in St. Moritz, Barbara Ann Scott of Ottawa, Ontario, is the first North American to win gold in figure skating. Canada regains its gold in hockey.

- William Lyon Mackenzie King, Canada's longest serving prime minister, resigns on November 15. He is succeeded by Louis St. Laurent.

1949

- Following a narrowly won referendum in July 1948 giving Newfoundlanders the choice between self-government or Confederation with Canada, Newfoundland officially becomes Canada's tenth province on March 31. In 2001, the province's name is officially changed to Newfoundland and Labrador.

- On April 4, Canada and 11 other nations sign a treaty creating the North Atlantic Treaty Organization (NATO), a military alliance.

- The Liberals under Louis St. Laurent win a majority in the federal election on June 27.

The 1950s

Korea, the Richard Riot, Suez Peacekeeping and No More Avro Arrow

1950

- The Korean War begins on June 25 when North Korea invades South Korea. Canada becomes involved as part of a United Nations force backing South Korea.

- An August strike by 130,000 railway workers against both CPR and CNR is the largest in Canadian history, shutting down the Canadian economy for a week. It ends when the government legislates the strikers back to work.

1951

- The census puts the Canadian population at 14,009,429 people.

- The Battle of Kapyong, fought in Korea April 24–25, is one of Canada's greatest military achievements. About 700 Canadian soldiers hold off a Chinese force of 5000 in defence of a crucial hill on the front line of the war.

- Princess Elizabeth, with her husband, the Duke of Edinburgh, makes her first royal visit to Canada from October 8 to November 12. Mere months later, she will be queen.

1952

- On January 24, Vincent Massey becomes the first Canadian-born Governor General of Canada.

- On February 6, Elizabeth II becomes queen following the death of her father, King George VI. As of September 2015, she is the longest-reigning British monarch.

- Canada once again wins hockey gold at the Winter Olympics in Oslo, but it will prove to be their last gold medal performance for 50 years.

- The CBC's first television station goes on the air in Montréal on September 6, followed two days later by its Toronto station.

1953

- The National Library of Canada is established on January 1. In 2004, it will join with the National Archives of Canada to become Library and Archives Canada. The national library's mandate is to "acquire, preserve, promote and provide access to the published heritage of Canada for all Canadians."

- On July 27, an armistice is signed between North and South Korea, and the combat phase of the war is over. Canadians continue to serve a peacekeeping role in Korea until 1957.

- Louis St. Laurent's Liberals win another majority in the federal election on August 10.

1954

- The Toronto Subway opens its first 12-station segment on March 30. It is the first rapid transit system in Canada.

- On August 10, construction begins on the St. Lawrence Seaway. It is a joint project between Canada and the United States. By 1959, it is open to commercial traffic.

- Marilyn Bell, a Toronto swimmer, is just 16 years old when she becomes the first person to swim across Lake Ontario. Starting at Youngstown, New York, on September 8, she reaches Toronto 21 hours later, where a huge crowd is waiting to congratulate her.

- Hurricane Hazel strikes the Toronto area in October, causing devastation. The aftermath includes 81 people dead, nearly 1900 families homeless and up to $100 million in damages.

1955

- On March 17, a riot breaks out in Montréal over the suspension of the Montréal Canadiens' star player, Maurice Richard, just before the playoffs. The "Richard Riot" is one of the worst in Canadian history, but it is seen as an important event in Québec's nationalist movement.

- Canada's Sports Hall of Fame opens in Toronto on August 24 as Canada's national museum of sport. In 2011, it is relocated to Calgary.

1956

- The Pipline Debate is one of the biggest in parliamentary history, taking place from May 8 to June 6. The Liberals want to build a pipeline to carry natural gas from Alberta to central Canada with TransCanada Pipelines as the builder. Over various concerns from the opposition including cost and ownership, the bill is passed and construction begins. Two years later, the pipeline is complete.

- Suez Crisis: Tension over control of the Suez Canal in Egypt had been growing and finally comes to a head on October 31, when Britain and France begin bombing the Canal Zone, trying to force Egypt to retreat. Lester B. Pearson, Canada's secretary of state for external affairs and head of Canada's delegation to the United Nations, puts forth his idea for a UN peacekeeping force, and member nations vote overwhelmingly in favour of it. Britain and France withdraw from the Canal Zone without being defeated, and a UN Emergency Force, led by Canadian General E.L.M. Burns, takes over in late November. Pearson will win the Nobel Peace Prize the following year.

1957

- The Canada Council for the Arts is founded on March 28 with the mandate to "foster and promote the study and enjoyment of, and the production of works in, the arts."

- Canadians are in the mood for change, and John Diefenbaker's Conservative Party wins a minority in the federal election on June 10, defeating Louis St. Laurent and the long-established Liberals. Diefenbaker is sworn in as prime minister on June 21.

- On August 1, Canada and the U.S. announce the North American Air Defense Agreement (NORAD) as an effort to join air forces to fight the Cold War. The name has since been changed to the North American Aerospace Defense Command, and though somewhat different in scope, the pact remains in effect.

- Nat Taylor creates the first dual movie theatre, showing two different movies in one location in Ottawa. Taylor will go on to build the first 18-screen Cineplex in 1979, and multi-plexes are now the norm.

1958

- Having called an election in the hopes of cementing his status as prime minister, Diefenbaker wins the largest majority thus far in Canadian history on March 31.

- In the world's largest planned non-nuclear peacetime explosion to date, Ripple Rock is blown up off the coast of BC on April 5, making the Seymour Narrows much safer for shipping traffic.

- A dam holding back the St. Lawrence River near Cornwall, Ontario, is demolished on July 1, leading to the flooding of nine communities and the forced relocation of 6500 people to facilitate new hydroelectric power plants along the St. Lawrence Seaway. The Lost Villages are still remembered today.

1959

- On February 20, the Diefenbaker government cancels the Avro Arrow project. Touted as potentially the world's fastest and most advanced interceptor aircraft, mounting costs and falling demand led to the controversial cancellation.

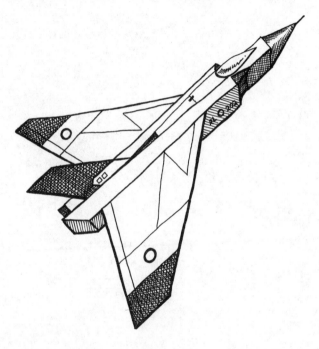

- The longest royal tour in Canadian history takes Queen Elizabeth to every province and territory over the course of the summer.

- In November, the Board of Broadcast Governors, created the previous year, announces new rules for Canadian content on television.

The 1960s

Quiet Revolution, Tim Hortons, the Maple Leaf Flag and Canada's Centennial

1960

- On March 31, the government grants Canadian First Nations the unconditional right to vote in federal elections. The Inuit had been enfranchised in 1950, but ballot boxes were not made readily accessible until 1962.

- On August 10, the Canadian Bill of Rights is Canada's first law to protect human rights and freedoms.

- The Quiet Revolution begins in Québec. It is a time of rapid social, cultural, economic and political change under the provincial Liberal Party and coincides with a rise in nationalist sentiment.

1961

- The census puts the Canadian population at 18,238,247 people.

- Tommy Douglas is elected leader of the newly formed New Democratic Party (NDP) on August 3. The NDP unites the former Co-operative Commonwealth Federation (CCF) and the Canadian Labour Congress as the major federal socialist party. Douglas is the former premier of Saskatchewan, having led that province for the previous 17 years.

- On October 1, CTV begins broadcasting. It is Canada's second major television network.

1962

- Ellen Fairclough, minister of citizenship and immigration and the first woman appointed to the cabinet, introduces an act on January 19 to eliminate discrimination based on race, colour or nationality from Canada's immigration policy.

- John Diefenbaker loses his majority in the federal election on June 18 but manages to hold onto a minority to remain prime minister.

- The Trans-Canada Highway officially opens on July 30. Canadians can now drive from coast to coast on the longest national highway in the world.

- During the Cuban Missile Crisis in October, Prime Minister Diefenbaker initially resists the request by U.S. President Kennedy to move Canadian forces to a higher alert. It is a controversial decision and contributes to the collapse of Diefenbaker's government.

1963

- Lester B. Pearson's Liberals win a minority in the federal election on April 8, defeating Diefenbaker's Conservatives. Pearson is sworn in as prime minister on April 22.

- *Hinterland Who's Who*, a series of one-minute vignettes about Canadian wildlife, begins airing on Canadian television. The series was commissioned by the Canadian Wildlife Service and produced by the National Film Board.

1964

- In April, Social Insurance Numbers (SIN) take effect in Canada as a personal identifier for most financial and service programs administered by the government.

- Also in April, hockey player Tim Horton opens his first coffee and doughnut shop in Hamilton, Ontario. It is so successful that he decides to expand it into a franchise, and the rest is history. Although Tim Hortons has been foreign-owned since 1995, it is part of the Canadian identity.

- Marshall McLuhan, an English professor at the University of Toronto, publishes *Understanding Media*, changing the way many people think about mass media.

The medium is the message.
–M. McLuhan

1965

- On February 15, Canada's new national flag, the Maple Leaf, is raised for the first time. An all-parties committee had voted for the design the previous year, and after months of debate, the flag was approved by the House of Commons and the Senate. The maple leaf is now an emblem for all Canadians.

- Lester Pearson and the Liberal Party win a second consecutive minority government in the federal election on November 8.

1966

- On January 1, the Canada Pension Plan (CPP) comes into effect. The compulsory program is intended to help Canadians avoid poverty in retirement.

- The Medical Care Act extends health coverage to every Canadian. Tommy Douglas is instrumental in getting the act passed. During his time as premier of Saskatchewan, he instituted government-funded health insurance. As leader of the federal NDP, he pushed Pearson's government to adopt a federal plan. Douglas is recognized as the Father of Medicare in Canada.

1967

- The Order of Canada is established on April 17 to recognize outstanding Canadians.

- On May 2, the Toronto Maple Leafs defeat the Montréal Canadiens to win the Stanley Cup. The 1966–1967 season is the last in the Original Six era, and the Leafs have not won a league championship since.

- July 1: Canada celebrates its centennial year with activitites and events across the country.

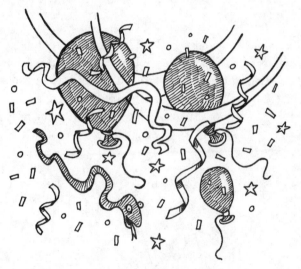

- Expo 67 in Montréal is one of Canada's biggest centennial celebrations. Countries around the world participate in the World's Fair, held from April 27 to October 29, and it is attended by more than 50 million people. It is a great success and stirs national pride in Canada.

1968

- On February 1, the Canadian Army, Royal Canadian Navy and Royal Canadian Air Force are dissolved as separate entities and merged in a single service: the Canadian Forces. Unification is never popular within the forces, and by 2014, the army, navy and air force are basically separate once more.

- The Canadian Radio-television and Telecommunications Commission (CRTC) is established on April 1 with the mandate to "ensure that broadcasting and telecommunications systems serve the Canadian public."

- Pierre Elliott Trudeau and the Liberals win a majority in the federal election on June 25. Trudeau had won leadership of the Liberal Party and been appointed prime minister following the resignation of Lester Pearson in April. The excitement generated by Pierre Trudeau's entry into the leadership race of the Liberal Party of Canada is dubbed "Trudeaumania."

- Originally named the Husky Tower, the Calgary Tower opens to the public on June 30. It was built to celebrate Canada's Centennial. It weighs 10,900 tonnes, and 60 percent of the structure is underground.

1969

- The Montréal Expos play their first home game on April 14. The baseball team is the first Canadian team admitted to U.S.-based Major League Baseball. The team will be relocated to Washington, DC, following the 2004 season.

- The Official Languages Act of July 7 makes both English and French the official languages of Canada. New Brunswick is the only province to follow suit; all other provinces retain English as their official language, except Québec, in which French is the only language.

The 1970s

Metric Conversion, the October Crisis, Hockey Supremacy and NHL Expansion

1970

- The slow conversion to the metric system of weights and measures begins with the release of the "White Paper on Metric Conversion in Canada" in January and continues through the early 1980s. Today, many Canadians still use a combination of the imperial and metric systems.

- The Vancouver Canucks enter the NHL in a league expansion on May 22. They play their first game on October 9.

- October Crisis: The Front de Liberation du Québec (FLQ) has been causing trouble in Québec since 1963, using violence to further their quest for an independent Québec. On October 5, 1970, FLQ members kidnap British trade commissioner James Cross in Montréal. On October 10, even as Québec officials are meeting FLQ demands, a separate cell kidnaps Pierre Laporte, Québec's minister of immigration and labour. Premier Robert Bourassa calls on the federal government for help, which leads Prime Minister Trudeau to invoke the War Measures Act on October 16, and the FLQ is outlawed. The next day, Laporte is found dead. Cross is discovered and eventually released in December. The use of the War Measures Act remains controversial; some view it as excesssive. Following the October Crisis, the separatist movement in Québec becomes more democratic.

1971

- Canada's first nuclear energy power plant begins operation in Pickering, Ontario, on April 5. The CANDU (Canada Deuterium Uranium) reactor is a uniquely Canadian technology that several countries around the world now use to generate electricity.

- The census puts the Canadian population at 21,568,305 people.

- The majority of new immigrants are of non-European ancestry for the first time. Prime Minister Trudeau declares his commitment to the principle of multiculturalism, aiming to protect and promote diversity while supporting Canada's two official languages and protecting Aboriginal rights.

1972

- In September, it's Canada vs. the Soviet Union in the Summit Series to decide hockey supremacy. The first seven games result in three wins each and a tie. The eighth and deciding game on September 28 draws the largest Canadian TV audience on record to watch Paul Henderson score the winning goal for Canada.

- Pierre Trudeau's Liberals win only a minority in the federal election on October 30.

- Anik A1 is launched on November 9. The satellite, operated by Telesat Canada, is the world's first domestic communications satellite in orbit.

1973

- The first federal government-authorized lottery in Canada is announced. Proceeds will go to fund the Montréal Summer Olympics, coming in 1976, and to develop amateur sport in participating provinces.

- Oil prices rise steeply, creating an economic boom in Alberta.

1974

- Two lieutenant-governor firsts happen in Canada. On January 17, Pauline McGibbon becomes the first woman appointed to the position, in Ontario; and on July 2 in Alberta, Ralph Steinhauer is the first Aboriginal person to hold the office.

- On May 23, the RCMP announces that it will begin accepting women into the force as regular police officers. The first troop of 32 women recruits arrives in Regina in September for training, and they graduate on March 3, 1975. Today, approximately one-fifth of RCMP officers are women.

- Pierre Trudeau and the Liberal Party win a majority government in the federal election on July 8.

1975

- The beaver, the most important animal to the fur trade that shaped early Canada, is made an official emblem of Canada on March 24.

- On November 10, the SS *Edmund Fitzgerald*, an American freighter, sinks in a storm on Lake Superior, taking her crew of 29 with her. The ship is the largest ever to go down in the Great Lakes and inspires a song by Canadian Gordon Lightfoot the following year. "The Wreck of the *Edmund Fitzgerald*" remains one of Lightfoot's biggest hits.

1976

- On June 26, the CN Tower opens to the public. At 553 metres high, the communications tower is the tallest freestanding structure in the world until 2007. In 1995, the American Society of Civil Engineers named the CN Tower one of the seven wonders of the modern world.

- Montréal is the first Canadian city to host the Olympic Games, in this case the Summer Olympics. Although expensive, the venture is a success. Canada wins 11 medals, far more than in recent Summer Games. It must have been the hometown crowd cheering them on.

- *Second City Television* (*SCTV*) premiers on Global Television. The sketch comedy show features several famous Canadian comedians including John Candy, Dave Thomas and Catherine O'Hara.

1977

- On January 1, Canada extends its Exclusive Economic Zone (EEZ) to 200 nautical miles offshore in an attempt to control its fishery. The now-standard EEZ boundary is formally adopted by the United Nations in 1982.

- Via Rail is created on February 28 as a crown corporation to take over passenger train service in Canada from Canadian Pacific and Canadian National.

- The Toronto Blue Jays play their first Major League Baseball game on April 7. They are the second, and now only, Canadian team in the league.

1978

- In August, Edmonton, Alberta, hosts the largest Commonwealth Games yet, with 1500 athletes from 46 countries competing and 10,000 local volunteers. Canada is the top medal winner, including 45 gold medals.

- On September 15, workers at the Sudbury, Ontario, INCO nickel plant go on strike. The strike will last until June 7, 1979, making it the longest strike in Canadian history until the strike of 2009–10 by workers at the same plant.

1979

- Joe Clark and the Conservatives win a minority in the federal election on May 22, defeating Pierre Trudeau. When he is sworn in on June 4, Clark becomes Canada's youngest prime minister. However, after a non-confidence motion on December 13, he is forced to call a new election for early 1980.

- David Suzuki takes over as host of *The Nature of Things*. Suzuki is perhaps Canada's best-known scientist and environmentalist.

- The Edmonton Oilers, Winnipeg Jets and Québec Nordiques join the NHL as part of an expansion. The next year, the Calgary Flames are Canada's seventh NHL team. While the Oilers and Flames franchises are still going strong, the Nordiques were sold and relocated to Denver in 1995, becoming the Colorado Avalanche, and the Jets were sold and moved to Phoenix in 1996, becoming the Coyotes. Winnipeg fans rejoiced when the Atlanta Thrashers were relocated to Winnipeg in 2011, with the Jets name reinstated.

The 1980s

Terry Fox, Canada in Space, the Constitution and Gretzky Gone

1980

- Pierre Trudeau and the Liberals win a narrow majority in the federal election on February 18, defeating Joe Clark. Although he has almost no support in the west, Trudeau is once again Canada's prime minister.

- After bone cancer causes him to lose his right leg, Terry Fox begins his Marathon of Hope on April 12 in St. John's, Newfoundland, to raise money for cancer research. He runs the equivalent of a marathon every day, gaining support along the way. He has reached Thunder Bay, Ontario, when he is forced to stop on September 1 because the cancer has spread to his lungs. He will die less than a year later on June 28, 1981. Terry Fox raised $24 million before his death, and since then, the Terry Fox Foundation has carried on fundraising in his name, ensuring a lasting legacy for one of Canada's greatest heroes.

- Québec votes "no" to sovereignty in a referendum on May 20.

- On July 1, "O Canada" officially becomes Canada's national anthem.

- On October 28, the Liberals introduce the National Energy Program, which aims to take control of the oil industry in Canada and redistribute Alberta's oil wealth. It is a short-lived program that mainly succeeds in further alienating western Canadians from central Canada in general and the federal Liberal Party in particular.

1981

- The census puts the Canadian population at 24,343,177 people.

- West Edmonton Mall, once the world's largest and still North America's largest shopping centre, opens Phase 1 on September 15. By the time Phase 3 is open in 1985, it is a major tourist attraction and remains so today.

- The Canadarm first goes to space aboard the shuttle *Columbia* on November 13. The robotic arm proved invaluable over its 30-year career with NASA, establishing Canada as a leader in space robotics. Canadarm2 launched in April 2001 and currently operates on the International Space Station.

1982

- On April 17, Queen Elizabeth signs the Constitution Act, finally completing the process of Canadian independence. The act, which patriated the Constitution in Canada, allows Canadians to amend the Constitution without getting approval from Britain.

- Canada's new Constitution includes the Canadian Charter of Rights and Freedoms, which gives individual Canadians certain inviolable rights and freedoms, with some limitations. The charter supercedes the 1960 Bill of Rights.

- Gilles Villeneuve, Canada's first champion Formula One auto racer, dies in a crash in Belgium on May 8. Despite his career being cut short, he is still considered one of Canada's best.

1983

- On July 23, an Air Canada flight from Montréal to Edmonton is forced to make an emergency landing at Gimli, Manitoba, when it runs out of fuel. The problem is caused by a miscalculation in the amount of fuel needed, resulting from confusion between metric and imperial measurements. The pilot managed to glide the plane to a safe landing, narrowly avoiding disaster. The "Gimli Glider" incident is one hiccup in an otherwise fairly smooth, though long, metric conversion process.

- A great white shark is caught off the west coast of P.E.I. in August. At 5.2 metres long, it is the second largest great white ever measured.

1984

• On May 14, Jeanne Sauvé becomes Canada's first female Governor General.

• Canadian entertainment giant Cirque de Soleil, the world's largest theatrical production company, is founded on June 16 in Baie-St-Paul, Québec, by former street performers Guy Laliberté and Gilles St-Croix.

• Brian Mulroney and the Conservatives win the largest majority to date in the federal election on September 4. Trudeau had retired in June, and Mulroney ran a nearly flawless campaign against John Turner, Trudeau's seccessor. Mulroney is sworn in as prime minister on September 17.

• On October 5, Marc Garneau is the first Canadian in space. He is an astronaut aboard the shuttle *Challenger*.

1985

• Rick Hansen begins his Man in Motion tour on March 21. The well-known wheelchair athlete is inspired by his friend Terry Fox to raise money for spinal cord research, rehabilitation and wheelchair sports by travelling 40,000 kilometres, a distance equivalent to once around the world. Over the course of two years, he wheels himself through 34 countries before starting across Canada, raising more than $20 million along the way.

- The Royal Tyrrell Museum of Palaeontology opens in Drumheller, Alberta, on September 25. It is Canada's most famous museum dedicated to prehistoric life and includes a full Tyrannosaurus rex skeleton.

- The deadliest airplane accident to date on Canadian soil occurs on December 12 when Arrow Air Flight 1285 crashes shortly after takeoff from Gander, Newfoundland, killing all 256 people on board.

1986

- Expo 86 in Vancouver draws 20 million visitors. The popular international exposition is part of Vancouver's centennial celebration and runs from May 2 to October 13.

- On October 6, Canada is awarded the Nansen Medal by the United Nations in recognition of its contribution to refugee protection.

1987

- The Meech Lake Accord is Prime Minister Mulroney's attempt to gain Québec's support for the new Constitution. He strikes an agreement with the provinces on April 30 that gives them more power and additionally declares Québec a "distinct society." However, over the next three years, the deal unravels before it can be ratified.

- The "loonie" is introduced on June 30, replacing the one-dollar bill.

- Canada and the United States sign a bilateral free trade agreement in October that will come into effect January 1, 1989. It is the precursor to the North American Free Trade Agreement of 1994.

1988

- Calgary hosts the Winter Olympics in February. These Winter Games are the largest yet and are famous for the first Jamaican bobsled team and for British ski jumper Michael "Eddie the Eagle" Edwards.

- The hockey world is rocked when Wayne Gretzky is traded from Edmonton to the Los Angeles Kings on August 9. Oilers owner Peter Pocklington becomes the most hated man in Edmonton. Gretzky had led the Oilers to four Stanley Cups in five years, and although the Oilers will win one more cup in 1990, the Gretzky trade is the beginning of the end for the Oilers dynasty.

- On September 24, Ben Johnson, Canadian track superstar, wins the 100 metre sprint at the Summer Olympics in Seoul in a record time. Canada's hero quickly falls from grace when he tests positive for steroids and is stripped of his gold medal three days later.

- Brian Mulroney and the Conservatives win a second majority in the federal election on November 21 after running a campaign backing his free trade agreement with the U.S.

1989

• The Canadian Space Agency is created on March 1 with the mandate to promote the peaceful use and development of space through science and technology for the social and economic benefit of Canadians.

• On May 25, the Calgary Flames defeat the Montréal Canadiens to win their first, and to date only, Stanley Cup.

• Audrey McLaughlin is elected leader of the NDP on December 2, making her the first woman to lead a national political party in Canada.

• In what will become known as the Montréal Massacre, 14 women are shot and killed at Montréal's Ecole Polytechnique on December 6. It is a shocking act of violence against women.

The 1990s

The Oka Crisis, Cod Collapse, the Québec Referendum and Nunavut

1990

- In March, Canada wins the first Women's World Hockey Championship.

- Oka Crisis: When the town of Oka announces plans to expand onto land claimed by the Mohawk as sacred, Mohawk protesters set up a barricade, preventing construction from going ahead. The July through September standoff between protesters and police results in one police officer killed and the armed forces being called in. It comes to an end when the federal government agrees to purchase the land and prevent future development.

1991

- On January 1, the Goods and Services Tax (GST) comes into effect over much protest.

- The census puts the Canadian population at 27,296,856 people.

1992

- On January 22, Dr. Roberta Bondar is the first Canadian woman in space, aboard the shuttle *Discovery*.

- A moratorium on the Atlantic cod fishery comes into effect on July 2. The collapse of the fishery has grave economic consequences on the east coast of Canada.

- After the failure of the Meech Lake Accord in 1990, the Charlottetown Accord of August 28 is another attempt by the Mulroney government to obtain Québec's consent to the Constitution Act of 1982. Although it has the support of the federal and provincial governments, Canadians reject it in a referendum on October 26.

- The Ottawa Senators play their first game on October 8 after entering the NHL in a league expansion. The original Ottawa Senators team was a charter member of the NHL in 1917 but folded in the early 1930s.

1993

- On June 25, Kim Campbell becomes the first female prime minister in Canada. She had won the Conservative leadership after Brian Mulroney announced his resignation in February.

- Jean Chrétien and the Liberal Party win a majority in the federal election on October 25, handing Kim Campbell and the Conservatives their worst-ever defeat when that party is reduced to two seats. Chrétien is sworn in as prime minister on November 4.

1994

- On January 1, the North American Free Trade Agreement (NAFTA) comes into effect between Canada, the United States and Mexico, creating one of the largest free trade zones in the world.

- Victoria, BC, hosts the Commonwealth Games in August. Canada again does well, competing against 65 other nations.

- Hockey is named Canada's official winter sport; lacrosse is Canada's official summer sport.

1995

- Another referendum on Québec sovereignty on October 30 results in a narrow win for the "no" side: 50.58 percent. The country will remain intact, but the federal government does officially recognize Québec as a "distinct society" within Canada.

- Both the Toronto Raptors and the Vancouver Grizzlies play their first games in the National Basketball Association (NBA). The Grizzlies will be sold and moved to Memphis in 2001. Toronto is currently the only Canadian city to host major professional franchises in basketball, baseball, football, soccer and hockey.

1996

- The two-dollar coin enters circulation on February 19 to replace the two-dollar bill and is quickly nicknamed the "toonie."

- During the Summer Olympics in Atlanta, Donovan Bailey is Canada's sprinting hero when he wins the 100-metre race in a record time of 9.84 seconds.

- The last residential school in Canada closes in November. The schools, in operation since the 1880s across Canada, had been a government-sponsored attempt to assimilate Aboriginal children into Euro-Canadian culture, with disastrous consequences for the children and their communities. In 2008, Prime Minister Stephen Harper offered an apology on behalf of the Canadian government to all former students of the schools, in addition to the Indian Residential Schools Settlement Agreement of 2007.

1997

- The Confederation Bridge opens to traffic on May 31, connecting Prince Edward Island to New Brunswick. It is the longest bridge in the world to cross over ice-covered water.

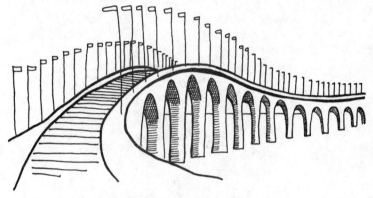

- Jean Chrétien and the Liberals win a second consecutive majority in the federal election on June 2.

- Lilith Fair, organized by Canadian singer-songwriter Sarah McLachlan, is the summer's biggest-selling concert tour and raises millions for various charities.

1998

- A major ice storm hits the St. Lawrence valley in January. It causes as many as 35 deaths, 945 injuries and the temporary displacement of 600,000 people, as well as power outages for millions of residents and a financial cost in the billions. It is one of Canada's worst natural disasters.

- Canada's first diamond mine opens in the Northwest Territories in October. By 2003, Canada is the third largest diamond producer in the world.

1999

- On April 1, Nunavut officially becomes Canada's third territory in a division of the Northwest Territories.

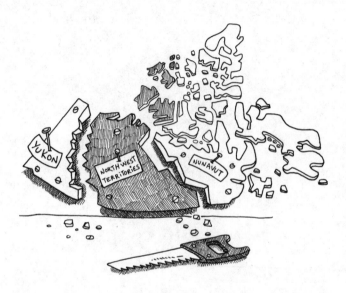

- The Nisga'a people of British Columbia sign a historic treaty with the federal and provincial governments resolving their claim to their traditional lands and granting them the right to self-government. The treaty officially came into effect on May 11, 2000, setting a precedent for other First Nations across Canada to make their own land claims.

The 2000s

Afghanistan, BlackBerry and Marriage Equality

2000

- The Clarity Act, passed in June, makes clear the conditions that must be met for Québec, or any other province, to secede from Canada. In effect, it is now more difficult to separate.

- Jean Chrétien and the Liberals win a third consecutive majority in the federal election on November 27.

2001

- The census puts the Canadian population at 30,007,094 people.

- In July, Canada becomes the first country to legalize marijuana for medicinal use.

- In October, Canada announces that it will send soldiers to Afghanistan as part of a U.S.-led coalition to capture members of al-Qaeda and overthrow the Taliban regime. This action is in response to the terrorist attacks on September 11 in the United States. Over the next 10 years, Canadian forces fight to establish peace and rebuild Afghanistan. In 2011, Canada ends its combat role but stays on to help train Afghan soldiers and police and to help rebuild the country. In 2014, the last Canadian soldiers leave Afghanistan. Over the course of the mission, more than 40,000 Canadians served; 158 were killed and more than 600 were wounded.

2002

- February's Winter Olympics in Salt Lake City are Canada's most successful showing to date. Both the men's and women's teams win hockey gold, putting Canada back on top of the hockey world. Clara Hughes is the first Canadian to win medals in both the Summer and Winter Olympics, for cycling in the 1996 Atlanta Games and for speed skating in Salt Lake City. Jamie Salé and David Pelletier win gold for pairs figure skating after a judging scandal resulted in them originally being awarded silver.

- Parliament under Prime Minister Chrétien formally ratifies the Kyoto Protocol on December 17, committing Canada to reducing its greenhouse gas emissions as per the conditions of the international agreement. However, after failing to meet its reduction targets, coupled with non-compliance of other major emissions-producing countries, Canada announces its withdrawal from Kyoto in 2011.

2003

- The first legal same-sex marriage in Canada takes place in Ontario on June 10.

- Paul Martin is sworn in as prime minister on December 12. He had become leader of the Liberal Party following the resignation of Jean Chrétien.

- Canadian company Research in Motion (RIM) releases the BlackBerry smartphone. Over the coming years, BlackBerry users rise exponentially worldwide before falling to competition from rival smartphone companies. The Canadian pioneer just couldn't keep up.

2004

- Paul Martin's Liberals win only a minority government in the federal election on June 28. The fall in voter confidence is blamed in part on the sponsorship scandal plaguing the Liberal Party.

- On October 17, CBC's *Greatest Canadian* series announces 10 finalists: Frederick Banting, Alexander Graham Bell, Don Cherry, Tommy Douglas, Terry Fox, Wayne Gretzky, John A. Macdonald, Lester Pearson, David Suzuki and Pierre Trudeau. On November 29, Tommy Douglas is revealed as Canada's vote for the Greatest Canadian.

2005

- The Civil Marriage Act is given royal assent on July 20, meaning that same-sex marriage is now legal nationwide.

- Satellite radio launches in Canada, vastly increasing the variety of stations Canadians can access.

2006

- Stephen Harper and the Conservative Party win a minority in the federal election on January 23, defeating Paul Martin's Liberals. Harper is sworn in as prime minister on February 6.

- The movie *Bon Cop Bad Cop*, a darkly comedic action thriller, is released in August. The fully bilingual film is a huge commercial success in Canada, proving that English and French can peacefully coexist.

2007

- After a pair of Russian submarines descend to the seabed under the North Pole and attempt to claim it for Russia in August, Canada's armed forces begin a series of military exercises in the Arctic in an attempt to display Canadian sovereignty in the North. The debate over control of resources and waterways in the Arctic is ongoing.

- On August 20, a human foot washes ashore in British Columbia. It is the beginning of an odd phenomenon. Over the coming years, several more feet are discovered on BC beaches, the latest in February 2016, but police have determined no foul play is involved.

2008

- After 40 years, CBC loses the rights to the *Hockey Night in Canada* theme song when contract negotiations break down in June. Canada's unofficial second national anthem is picked up by CTV for its TSN hockey broadcasts.

- Stephen Harper and the Conservatives retain a minority government in the federal election on October 14.

2009

- A research team from the University of Toronto discovers a widespread cyber-espionage network called GhostNet in March. China is behind the attacks, which compromise the computer systems of several governments worldwide.

- Guy Laliberté, co-founder of Cirque du Soleil, is Canada's first space tourist when he blasts off on September 30 for a 10-day stay at the International Space Station. He says the $35 million trip was worth every penny.

The 2010s

Political Shifts, No More Penny, Terror in Ottawa and the Sesquicentennial

2010

- Vancouver hosts the Winter Olympic Games in February, and they are Canada's most successful games to date. Canadian athletes win an unprecedented 14 gold medals (26 medals in total), including for both men's and women's hockey.

- Canada hosts the G8 and G20 global summits in June. The G20 Summit in Toronto is overshadowed by violent protests and the heavy-handed police response. Toronto police are held largely to blame for the fiasco.

2011

- The census puts the Canadian population at 33,476,688 people.

- Stephen Harper's Conservatives win a majority in the federal election on May 2, triggered as a result of a non-confidence vote March 25. The Liberals under Michael Ignatieff are reduced to third-party status, while Jack Layton's NDP rises to become the official opposition for the first time. Sadly, Layton's victory will be short-lived; he dies of cancer on August 22.

- Riots erupt in Vancouver on June 15 after the Canucks lose the Stanley Cup final to the Boston Bruins. The Canucks had been on the verge of their first NHL championship, and the disappointed fans took their frustration to the streets.

- Prince William and Duchess Kate, the Duke and Duchess of Cambridge, tour Canada from June 30 to July 8. The popular young couple is reinvigorating Canada's interest in Britain's royal family.

2012

- Canada rallies behind our women's soccer team at the Summer Olympics in London. On the verge of beating the Americans for the chance to play for gold, the team is given several controversial penalties, costing them the game in overtime. Captain Christine Sinclair is a sports hero for her performance. The team goes on to win bronze, and Sinclair is Canada's flag bearer at the closing ceremonies.

- Idle No More forms in November as a grassroots movement in protest of the federal government's plan to put the economy ahead of the environment and Aboriginal rights. Starting with four women in Saskatchewan, the movement quickly grows to attract thousands of supporters both nationally and internationally, galvanizing the Aboriginal community and stimulating discussion of both Aboriginal and environmental issues.

2013

- Costing more to make than it's worth, the penny is taken out of circulation on February 4.

- In March, Colonel Chris Hadfield becomes the first Canadian to command the International Space Station (ISS). With his use of Twitter to show the world what life is like on board the ISS, Hadfield becomes a global celebrity.

- On July 6, a freight train carrying crude oil derails and explodes in the town of Lac Megantic, Québec, killing 47 people and causing millions of dollars in damages. It is the worst rail disaster in Canada since Confederation.

- At a meeting of Canada's premiers on July 24, six of the 13 leaders are women. It is a landmark moment in Canadian politics.

2014

- At the Winter Olympics in Sochi, Canada remains on top of the world in hockey and curling, with both men's and women's teams taking gold in both sports. In all, Canadian athletes take home 25 medals.

- In September, a Parks Canada expedition finds HMS *Erebus*, one of two ships from the Franklin Expedition that went missing in the Arctic in 1846 while searching for the Northwest Passage. The second ship, HMS *Terror*, is discovered two years later, finally solving one of the most enduring mysteries of the Canadian North. The oral history and knowledge of the Inuit is instrumental in the discoveries.

- Corporal Nathan Cirillo is fatally shot while on ceremonial sentry duty at the war memorial in Ottawa on October 22. The shooter then enters the Centre Block parliament building, where members of parliament are holding caucus meetings. Several more shots are fired. Sergeant-at-Arms for the House of Commons Kevin Vickers is instrumental in wounding the shooter, and RCMP Constable Curtis Barrett takes the shot that kills Michael Zehaf-Bibeau. The terrorist act on home soil shakes Canadians nation-wide.

2015

- Political change comes at the federal level when Justin Trudeau's Liberal Party wins a majority in the federal election on October 19, defeating Stephen Harper and the Conservatives. The NDP falls from official opposition to third-party status. Trudeau is sworn in as prime minister on November 4.

- The Truth and Reconciliation Commission releases its final report in December. It includes 94 "calls to action" for all levels of government to work together to begin to repair the damage done to Aboriginals through the residential school system.

2016

- A wildfire forces the evacuation of 90,000 people in northern Alberta, including the entire city of Fort McMurray, in early May. Although firefighters manage to save the majority of the city, some 2400 buildings, most of them homes, are destroyed. Insurance claims are in the billions, making it the costliest natural disaster in Canadian history.

- The census taken on May 10 puts the Canadian population at 35,151,728 people.

- Canadians do well at the Summer Olympics in Rio de Janeiro, in particular 16-year-old swimmer Penny Oleksiak. Canada's youngest ever Olympic champion and the most successful Canadian athlete at a single Games comes home with four medals: one gold, one silver and two bronze. Sprinter Andre De Grasse is another exciting Canadian to watch, keeping up with the world's best on the track.

2017

- During the year, Canadians are encouraged to get out and get active with Canada's 150 Play List.

- July 1: Canada turns 150 years old. To celebrate, events are being held across the country. Parks Canada has waived admission fees to all national parks for the entire year. Happy Birthday, Canada!

ABOUT THE ILLUSTRATORS

Roger Garcia

Roger Garcia is a self-taught freelance illustrator based in Edmonton who works in acrylics, ink and digital media. His illustrations have been published in humour books, children's books, newspapers and educational material.

When Roger is not at home drawing, he can be seen facilitating cartooning workshops at various elementary schools, camps and local art events. Roger also enjoys participating with colleagues in art shows, painting murals in schools and public places.

Peter Tyler

Peter is a graduate of the Vancouver Film School Visual Art and Design, and Classical animation programs. Though his ultimate passion is in filmmaking, he is also intent on developing his draftsmanship and story-telling, with the aim of using those skills in future filmic misadventures.

Graham Johnson

Graham Johnson is an Edmonton-based illustrator and graphic designer. When he isn't drawing or designing, he...well...he's always drawing or designing! On the off-chance that you catch him not doing one of those things, he's probably cooking, playing tennis or poring over other illustrations.

Patrick Hénaff

Born in France, Patrick Hénaff is mostly self-taught and is a versatile artist who has explored a variety of mediums under many different influences. He now uses primarily pen and ink to draw and then processes the images on computer. He is particularly interested in the narrative power of pictures and tries to use them as a way to tell stories, whether he is working on comic pages, posters, illustrations, cartoons or concept art.

Craig Howrie

Craig is a self-taught artist. His line art has been used in local businesses' private events as well as a local comic book art anthology. He is also a songwriter working feverishly at a project to see the light of day hopefully within the next decade or so....

Djordje Todorovic

Djordje Todorovic is an artist/illustrator living in Toronto, Ontario. He first moved to the city to go to York University to study fine arts. It was there that he got a taste for illustrating while working as the illustrator for his college paper, *Mondo Magazine*. He has since worked on various projects and continues to perfect his craft. Aside from his artistic work, Djordje devotes his time volunteering at the Print and Drawing Centre at the Art Gallery of Ontario. When he is not doing that, he is out trotting the globe. He has illustrated three other books.

ABOUT THE AUTHOR

A.H. Jackson

Alan Jackson believes that, in the twine of life, there are two special genes unique to humankind—hope and humour—and he thinks we should all turn to the funny side of life in the face of adversity. He must have quite the sense of humour, then, since he's been struck by lightning five times!

Alan is prolific writer of nonfiction and a creator of worlds in the fiction realm. Alan lives in Toronto with a wife named M and a squirrel called Mommy. He is the author of various Blue Bike titles, including *Weird Canadian Weather, Weird Ontario Weather, Weird Ontario Laws, Weird Facts About Toronto* and *Spectacular Canadians*.